My book

Story by Jenny Giles
Illustrations by Susy Boyer Rigby

I am looking for my book.

2

My book is not here.

Look!

Here is my elephant.

I am looking for my book.

My book is not up here.

Look!

Here is my monkey.

I am looking for my book.

My book is not down here.

Look!

Here is my tiger.

Look!

Here is my book.

Look at me.

I can read my book.